MAGIC
IN ART

ALEXANDER STURGIS

Belitha Press

Editor: **Ann Kay**

Designer: **Steve Bretel**

Picture researchers: **Dee Robinson, Juliet Duff**

Consultant: **Anthea Peppin**

All illustrations by Steve Bretel, except for p4: Kate Hirons
and p23 bottom left: Laura Andrew

First published in the UK in 1994 by

Belitha Press, London House, Great Eastern Wharf,
Parkgate Road, London SW11 4NQ

Reprinted in 1997

ISBN 1 85561 357 3 (Hardback)
ISBN 1 85561 534 7 (Paperback)

Printed in Hong Kong

British Library Cataloguing in Publication Data for this book is available
from the British Library

CONTENTS

BEFORE YOU READ ON...

You will see 'c' in front of some dates in this book – for example c1630. The c is short for *circa*. This is a Latin word that means 'about'.

 Captions with this kind of arrow in front of them are the main captions to the paintings. They tell you all about what a picture is called, when it was painted, and who painted it.

 Captions with a pointing hand in front of them get you to look closer – at one particular thing in a painting.

YOUR OWN FLICK-CARTOON

In the bottom left-hand corner of every other page, starting with the page opposite, you will see a black triangle with a mysterious picture inside it. Get hold of all the pages with your right hand and flick them quickly – so that you are flicking from the front of the book to the back – while watching these black triangles. A moving mini-cartoon magically appears. You could try making similar flick-cartoons of your own.

FOOLING THE EYE

For centuries, painters have deceived us into thinking that something is real and solid when it is really only a painted illusion.

Still Life with a Flower Garland and a Curtain, 1658, by Adriaen van der Spelt (c1630-1673) and Frans van Mieris (1635-1681) Nothing you can see here is real. Even the curtain is painted, drawn back to reveal a different painting underneath.

There is a very old tale about artists that is all about their ability to deceive. In ancient Greece there were two famous painters – Zeuxis and Parrhasius – who challenged each other to a contest. Zeuxis painted some grapes that were so realistic that birds flew up to peck at them. Certain that he would win, Zeuxis turned to his rival's painting. It seemed to be hanging behind a curtain. But when Zeuxis went to draw  it back, he discovered that it too was painted. Because Parrhasius had fooled a fellow artist, he won the contest.

Madonna and Child with Two Angels, c1480, by an unknown artist
Here the artist has carefully painted a very realistic torn effect around the outside of the picture. This fools us into thinking that the painting has just been unwrapped.

Can you spot where this is in the picture on the left?

Is what you see what you get?

All the paintings on these two pages use the same trick to fool the eye. The artists have painted things that look as if they are on top of the paintings, when in fact they are part of them. Everything you can see is simply paint. Of course, this sort of trick is much more difficult in a book. Or is it? Can you spot anything like this on these two pages?

DID YOU KNOW?

● The term used for paintings – or parts of paintings – that fool you into thinking that they are real is *trompe l'oeil*. This is French for 'deceive the eye'.

● There is a story that when the artist Cimabue saw a fly crawling across a painting by his famous pupil Giotto (1267-1337), he tried to brush it away – only to realize that it was paint.

Portrait of a Woman of the Hofer Family, c1500, by an unknown artist
It looks as if someone has photographed this painting just as a fly was crawling across it. In fact, the fly was always there – it is part of the painting. The painter of this picture may perhaps have been thinking of the story of the Italian artist Giotto, explained in the Did You Know? feature on the left.

5

THE ART OF DISGUISE

Artists have found all kinds of ways of disguising their paintings so that they can make objects appear or whole walls disappear.

One of the ways in which we recognize paintings is that they hang on walls. Because of this, artists can make pictures 'disappear' by putting them where we do not expect to find them. The artist who painted this violin on a door was trying to deceive us so that we would not realize that it was simply a picture.

Painted Violin, probably by Jan van der Vaart (1647-1721)
The violin is not real – but the door is. This door led into a music room.

☞ *In order to make the trick work, the panels of the door and the shadows cast by the violin have also been painted.*

The Hall of Perspectives, Villa Farnesina, Rome, 1517-1518, by Baldassare Peruzzi (1481-1536)
This is just part of a whole room painted by Peruzzi. The columns, sculpture, balcony and view do not actually exist. They are all painted on to a flat wall, to make the room seem bigger and grander than it actually is.

Letter Rack with Curtain, 1671-1672, by Cornelis N. Gysbrechts (c1610-1676)
The artist of this picture probably hoped that people would reach up and try to take out the letters – only to discover their mistake.

Where does the floor end and the wall begin? The artist has painted floor tiles on the bottom of the wall just like those on the real floor.

On the wall

Other artists have painted pictures where we would normally expect to see them – on walls – but they have still tricked us. For example, by painting a scene across a whole wall, artists can make the flat surface seem to disappear and turn into something else – like the picture above. Another trick is to paint pictures of things like notice-boards or letter racks that hang on walls with frames around them, just like paintings. At first glance, people might not recognize these as paintings at all.

DID YOU KNOW?

● Peruzzi, the artist who painted the Hall of Perspectives, was influenced by the wall paintings of ancient Rome. There is a famous story that the architecture painted on the walls of one room in ancient Rome was so realistic that birds tried to land on it – just as they tried to peck at the grapes in the story on page 4.

7

THE DISAPPEARING CEILING

The pictures on these pages are painted on ceilings. The artists have created scenes that make the ceilings seem to disappear.

☞ *This is a detail of the ceiling shown below. On this painted balcony there are several young women and some strange babies with wings. Some of the babies seem to have got their heads stuck in the holes of the balcony.*

The Italian painter Andrea Mantegna (c1431-1506) was one of the first artists to paint a 'hole' in a ceiling. The painting on this page was on the ceiling of a room in the palace of the wealthy and powerful Duke Lodovico Gonzaga of Mantua, Italy. When Lodovico and his courtiers looked up, they would have seen what seemed to be a balcony open to the sky.

▶ **From the ceiling of The Painted Room in the Ducal Palace, Mantua, 1465-1474, by Andrea Mantegna**
The illusion of this painting can never work completely in a book. But it works much better if you hold the book above your head and look up at it.

8

☞ *This is a detail from the ceiling on the right. It shows how Pozzo increased the illusion of soaring heights by painting fake columns and arches leading up to the painted sky. Can you see where this section is in the picture of the whole ceiling?*

▶ **Ceiling in the Church of Saint Ignatius, Rome, 1691-1694, by Andrea Pozzo (1642-1709)**
This ceiling shows Saint Ignatius being carried up to heaven on a cloud by a crowd of angels. People looking up at this must have imagined that he had just taken off from the very spot on which they were standing.

This is what you see if you have just entered the church and look up

THE EYES HAVE IT!

One of the ways we know that a painting is not real and is only an illusion is that paintings do not move. Or do they?

Look at the eyes of the Mona Lisa, on the opposite page. This was painted by the famous Italian artist, Leonardo da Vinci. Her eyes seem to stare at you wherever you are. This magic works with lots of portraits and you could also paint a picture that behaves in this mysterious way.

What is the secret?
If you paint the person looking straight at you, then their eyes always seem to stare at whoever is looking at the picture. This is because paintings are flat. Wherever you look at the Mona Lisa from, you always see both eyes and the front of her nose. If you walk round to the side of the painting you will not see the side of her face. You will always see the whole of both eyes looking straight at you.

DID YOU KNOW?

● Because it is so famous, lots of artists have painted versions of the *Mona Lisa* (Madame Lisa). The French artist Marcel Duchamp (1887-1968) gave her a moustache and a beard!

● The *Mona Lisa* was once a bigger painting, but it has been cut down. It used to be clearer that she was sitting in a chair on a balcony with columns. You can just make out the base of a column on the left of the painting.

Baldassare Castiglione, 1514-1515, by Raphael (1483-1520)

When the eyes in a portrait appear to move, the person in the picture almost springs to life. This painting is of a writer who wrote a poem about how lifelike his portrait seemed – his words are shown below.

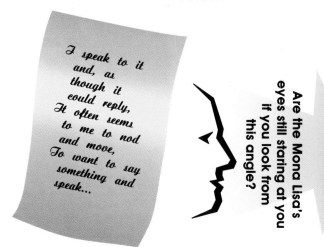

I speak to it and, as though it could reply, It often seems to me to nod and move, To want to say something and speak...

Are the Mona Lisa's eyes still staring at you if you look from this angle?

Mona Lisa, 1503-1506, by Leonardo da Vinci (1452-1519)

As you look at this picture, try holding the book further away from you. The Mona Lisa will still be looking at you. If you prop up the book and walk to the furthest corner of the room she still looks at you (if you can still see her). But are her eyes really moving?

☞ Can you see anything peculiar about the landscape in the background of this painting? It appears to be lower on the left than on the right. This helps to create an effect that seems to add some movement to the picture, making it come alive.

☞ The Mona Lisa seems so real – see how carefully her hands and each fold in her gown have been painted. What do you think the rest of her would have looked like? Try painting a picture that shows all of the Mona Lisa.

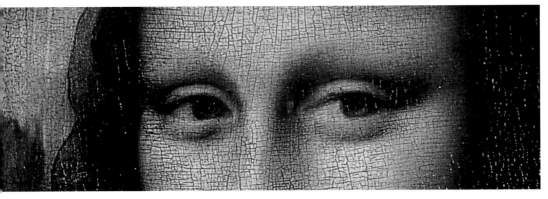

Are the Mona Lisa's eyes still staring at you if you look from this angle?

11

LOOKING THROUGH PAINTINGS

Paintings are simply flat pieces of wood, cloth or paper with paint on them. But some artists can create the illusion that you are looking right through a painting – as if you were looking through a window – at some view beyond.

Artists do this by using a system of drawing called perspective. This creates the illusion that an object painted on a flat surface is a solid, realistic shape. Using perspective involves drawing a framework of lines. With this, artists can make a picture look as though it is going back into real space, appearing smaller as it gets further away.

The Avenue, Middelharnis, 1689, by Meindert Hobbema (1638-1709)

Here, perspective gives the illusion that you really are looking straight down a path. One of the magical qualities of perspective is that, wherever you look at this painting from, the path always seems to be coming towards you.

☞ *This shows the main perspective structure of The Avenue. The red line represents the horizon – the line between sky and land. The dot in the centre of this line is the vanishing point. The lines in the picture go towards the vanishing point. We have marked some of these lines in blue – they are called orthogonals.*

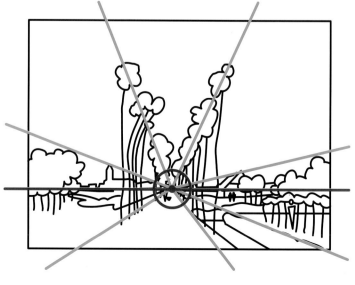

Q

In the painting on the opposite page, you feel that you are actually walking down the path, and that you might meet the man who is walking towards you at any minute. Why is this? (The answer is upside-down at the bottom of the page.)

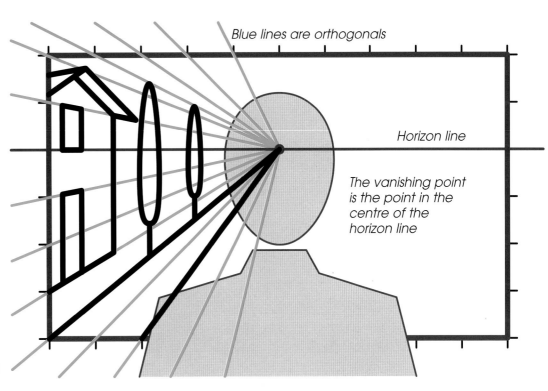

Blue lines are orthogonals

Horizon line

The vanishing point is the point in the centre of the horizon line

Try it yourself

Try drawing a simple picture in perspective. First plot the horizon line – the line between sky and land – right across the picture. Now plot the vanishing point, which is on the horizon line and opposite where you are looking at the view from. Lastly, plot 'orthogonals' – lines going back into the distance and meeting at the vanishing point.

Draw your own perspective picture

Choose a real or imaginary view that has an obvious horizon line. Draw a basic grid of perspective lines and then see how many things in the view will fit into your grid. If you are looking at a view from high up, the horizon line will be near the top of the picture. If you are low down, it will be near the bottom.

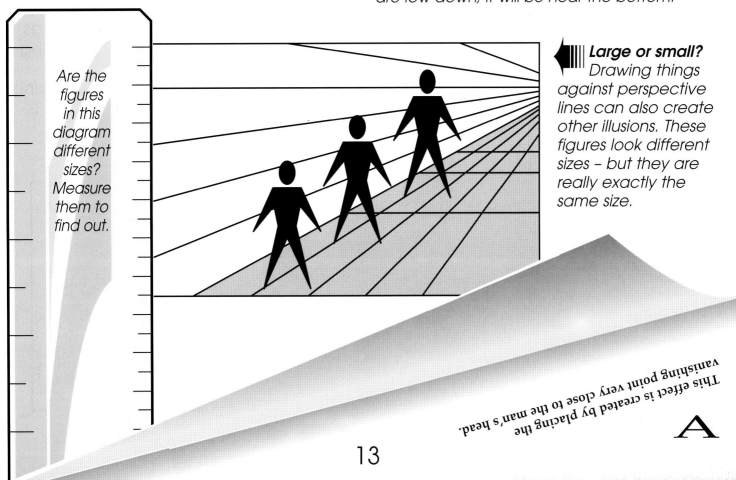

Are the figures in this diagram different sizes? Measure them to find out.

Large or small?

Drawing things against perspective lines can also create other illusions. These figures look different sizes – but they are really exactly the same size.

This effect is created by placing the vanishing point very close to the man's head.

A

13

PERSPECTIVE MAGIC

Some artists have understood the rules of perspective so well that they could play around with them to create impossible pictures like the print on the opposite page.

At first sight, this print, by the English artist William Hogarth (1697-1764), seems perfectly normal. There is no particular object or person that looks impossible. But look again – and you will see that almost everything about this picture is peculiar.

Making mistakes
In this print, Hogarth was trying to point out the sorts of mistakes that were often made by artists who did not understand the rules of perspective.

◀ False Perspective, 1754, by William Hogarth
This print is full of impossibilities. For example, the detail above looks normal until you find it in the picture. Then you see that the woman couldn't possibly be lighting this man's pipe. Other impossibilities are pointed out in the captions. How many more can you spot?

IMPOSSIBLE SHAPES
There are certain shapes you can draw that play perspective tricks similar to those in Hogarth's print. The triangle and cube below seem real. In fact, they could never exist. Can you see why not?

Make your own impossible shape
Look at the drawings on the right. 1. Trace this shape off on to a piece of paper. 2. Fold the paper as shown. How many columns does your impossible shape have?

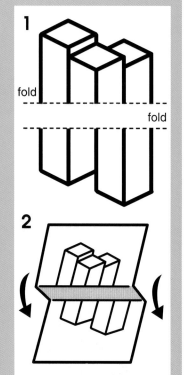

☞ *Look at the sign on the building. It seems to be behind the trees on the distant hill. And just how big is that bird on the top of the far tree?*

☞ *Shouldn't the sheep on the left of the print appear to get smaller as they walk further away around the corner?*

☞ *Look at the fisherman at the front of the picture. The fish on the end of his line is poking its head up in the distant river. And what is wrong with the tiles on which he is standing?*

15

THE IMPOSSIBLE WORLD

OF ESCHER

The Dutch printmaker M.C. Escher (1898-1972) is famous for his pictures of strange worlds in which nothing is as it seems.

To begin with Escher's pictures seem very real, and all the details are drawn very carefully. But look again. Gradually, you realize that his scenes could never exist. He achieves his clever effects by playing tricks with perspective.

Belvedere, 1958
In this picture, the ladder is somehow inside the building at the bottom and outside it at the top. And how do the arches and columns fit together?

In this detail, the man sitting on the bench is puzzling over an 'impossible cube'. He doesn't seem to realize that the building behind him is just as impossible.

In the print on the right, all the people seem to be going about their business in the same building. In fact, they are in different 'worlds' and couldn't possibly have anything to do with each other. Turn the picture round and look at it from each angle. How many 'worlds' are there – and how many people live in each one? (The answers are upside-down at the bottom of the page.)

Try turning the picture round to see how it works from each angle.

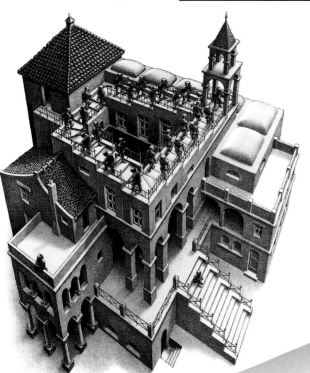

Relativity, 1953
At the top of this picture are two people walking side by side on the same staircase, but one of them is going up and the other is going down. How does this seem possible?

Ascending and Descending, 1960
Look closely at the top of this building. The hooded figures on the outside of the staircase are all walking up the stairs – but are they getting any higher?

There are three worlds: 1. When the picture is viewed straight on (five people live in this). 2. When seen from the left (five people live in this). 3. When seen from the right (six people live in this).

17

A

THE APPEARING PICTURE

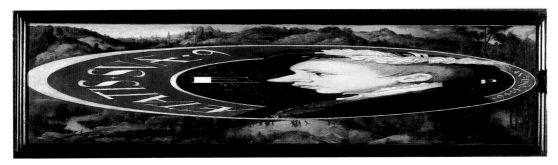

Some artists have used clever tricks with perspective to paint special pictures that are strangely stretched and distorted.

When you view one of these pictures straight on, it looks very odd. But if you look at it from a certain angle, the images suddenly appear clearly, as if from nowhere.

A trick of the eye
This trick is called 'anamorphosis' – a Greek word that means 'transform'. Look carefully at the painting above. It is a portrait of the English king, Edward VI, when he was a nine-year-old prince. You can just make out a face, but it is certainly not like a real person.

As if by magic...
Now hold the book upright and look at the picture from the side, with your eye as near to the page as you can get it. A realistic head magically appears. The artist has painted the portrait stretched out so that it only looks as it should when seen from the side.

Portrait of Prince Edward VI, 1546, by William Scrots (dates unknown)
The picture above shows the painting straight on. If you look at it from the side, you will see it corrected, as it appears in the picture on the left.

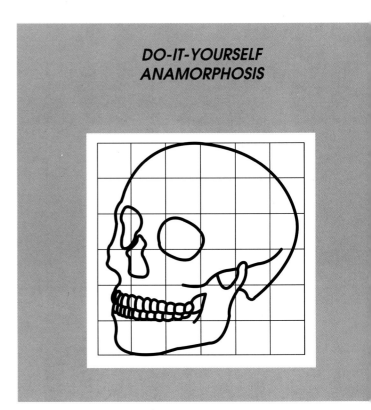

DO-IT-YOURSELF ANAMORPHOSIS

What is the strange object at the bottom of this picture? View from the side – as the arrow shows – to find out.

When you view the painting from the right-hand side, you will discover that this strange shape is actually a human skull. Anamorphosis can be used to hide messages in paintings. This hidden skull may carry a message about death.

Trace off these two grids (but not the actual drawings) on to another piece of paper. Now draw a simple picture – such as the example shown here – on to your square grid.

Next, transfer the picture, a square at a time, on to the squares of your long, triangular grid. Now view the picture on the long grid from the extreme right. It will magically look exactly as it did in your original drawing.

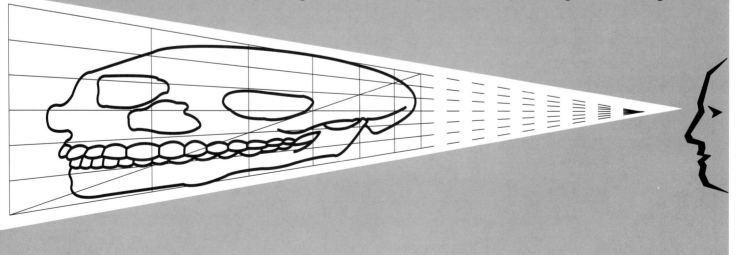

MIRROR IMAGES

The paintings shown here are confusing swirls of lines and colours. What do they mean? In fact, they have been painted like this on purpose.

When you place a cylindrical mirror in the centre of one of these kinds of pictures and look in the mirror, the painting comes alive. Artists painted pictures like this to show how clever they were at playing with the rules of perspective. The effect is a type of 'anamorphosis' – a distorted picture that is completely transformed when it is looked at in a special way. It is a variation of the trick that you saw on pages 18 and 19.

Anamorphic Painting of a Ship, probably 18th century, by an unknown artist
When you look at this painting you see nothing that you can recognize. But look in the mirror and the picture magically changes into a painting of an impressive ship.

Anamorphic Portrait of Charles II, painted after 1660, by an unknown artist
This is a portrait of the English king, Charles II. You can probably make out his face, with his moustache and long black hair, but it doesn't look anything like the king himself.

Where is the king? This portrait is painted so that you can only recognize the king by placing a cylindrical mirror in the middle of the painting. Try making your own mirror sheet (see box on the right) and find out whether you can make the portrait appear as it should, reflected in the sheet. (It is easier to find the king if you turn the book upside down before you put your sheet in place.)

MAKING A MIRROR SHEET

1. Cut out a piece of thick paper about 12cm high and 18cm wide. Now cut a piece of kitchen foil that is slightly larger. Use the thickest foil you can get. It must be very smooth – check that you can see your face in it. 2. Lay the paper on top of the foil. Fold the edges of the foil over and stick down with tape. 3. Now hold the sheet in a curved shape in the centre of the painting below. Curl it up more and less to see how the face appears and disappears.

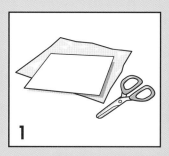

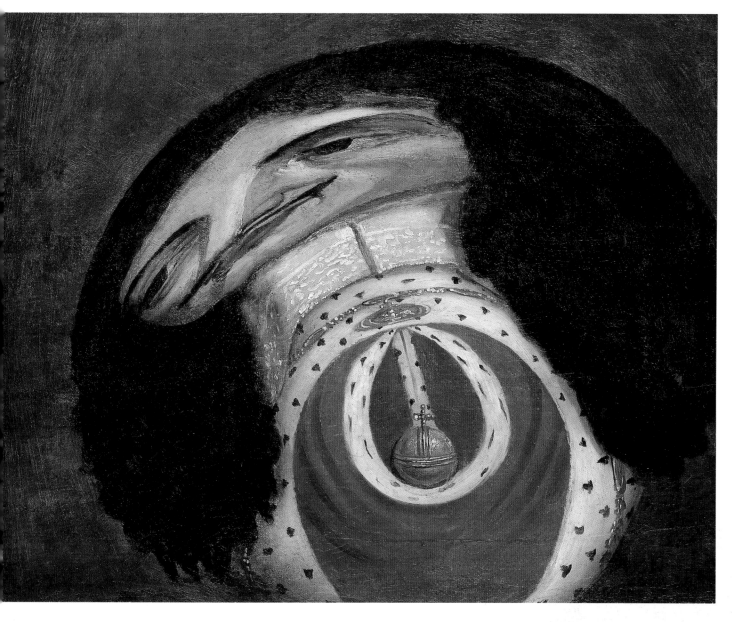

NOW YOU SEE IT...

Some pictures can change magically before your very eyes. They may appear to be two things at the same time, or seem to change from one thing into something totally different.

Look at the drawing on the right. What is it? Some people see it as a picture of a smart young woman. Others see it as an old, large-nosed woman in a cap. Can you see both people in this one picture? (If you can't, the caption underneath the picture explains how.) The young/old woman, and the rabbit/duck picture on the opposite page, are very well-known examples of images that you can see in different ways.

Young Woman/Old Woman
The two women in this picture are looking in completely different directions. The young woman is seen turning away from us and the old woman is looking down. The young woman's chin is the old woman's nose, her ear is the old woman's eye, and her neck-band is the old woman's mouth.

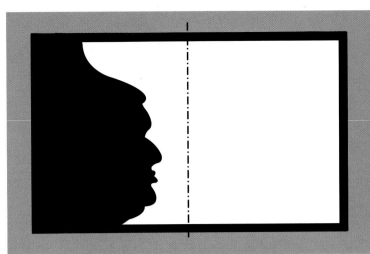

WHAT CAN YOU SEE?

Look at this face. Now try putting a mirror – or the foil sheet that you made on page 21 – along the dotted line, and angle it slightly. What you see in the mirror could either be two people facing each other or a white vase.

DID YOU KNOW?

- Rex Whistler, who drew the reversible head on the right, created a whole series of amusing 'two-in-one' portraits like this. They were used to advertise a well-known company and have become very famous. See what ideas you can come up with for drawing or painting your own reversible heads.

Reversible head, by Rex Whistler (1905-1944)

This man is unhappy because he is not certain whether his sweetheart loves him. What happens if you stand him on his head?

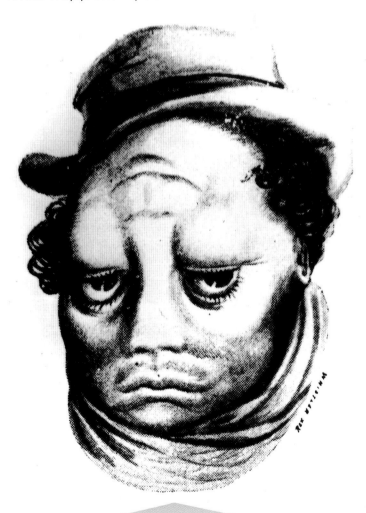

Who appears when you look from here?

Rabbit/Duck

One of the most famous of these changing pictures is this one of a rabbit. Or is it a duck? Are those pointed things ears – or a beak? Once you can see both the rabbit and the duck, you can make the picture change from one animal to another as you look at it.

23

ARCIMBOLDO – MAGICIAN OF PAINT

One of the greatest magician painters of all time was the Italian Giuseppe Arcimboldo (1527-1593).

Arcimboldo became very famous for painting magical, fantastical heads made up of fruits, vegetables, plants, books and all sorts of other objects. He was incredibly popular as a painter during his lifetime, and was even invited to paint at the courts of the Austrian emperors Ferdinand I, Maximilian II and Rudolph II.

Vertumnus, c1590
This portrait of Rudolph II is named after the ancient Roman god of vegetation.

How many different vegetables and fruits can you identify in this picture?

Fantastic festivals

Arcimboldo did not only paint pictures for the Austrian emperors. He also arranged and designed tournaments and festivals, in which members of the court appeared dressed in his fantastic costumes.

◀||| *The Vegetable Gardener, c1590*
There doesn't seem to be anything magical about this painting, but is a bowl of vegetables all that we can see? Where is the gardener?

Q
Have you found the vegetable gardener in the picture above yet? (The answer is upside-down at the bottom of the page.)

|||▶ *Winter, 1573*
This head is made from an old gnarled tree trunk, with fungus for lips and ivy for hair. These are all things you might expect to see in a wood in winter.

Hunt the detail
This fruit and vegetable are from Vertumnus. Can you find them in the painting? They do not grow at the same time of year. So Arcimboldo could never have made his head with real vegetables and fruits.

Look at the painting now that the book is upside-down. The vegetable gardener has magically appeared. His eyes are nuts, and his lips are two mushrooms.

A

SURREALISM

Some of the strangest and most fantastical pictures ever painted were made by a group of artists who began to work together in Paris in the 1920s. These artists called themselves the Surrealists.

 The Endless Enigma, 1938, by Salvador Dali (1904-1989)
It is difficult to work out what this strange painting – by the famous Spanish artist Dali – is supposed to show. You can make out some objects, but as you look at them, they seem to disappear and begin to change into something else.

The word 'sur' means 'on top of' in French, and 'beyond' when it is used at the beginning of English words. These artists invented the word Sur-realism to describe their work because what they painted was beyond what everyone thought of as being normal reality.

Dream worlds

Instead of trying to paint pictures that showed the real world, the Surrealists wanted to conjure up the world of the imagination – where anything at all is possible. Many of the magical things that they painted were inspired by their dreams. The Surrealists believed that dreams contained hidden meanings.

DID YOU KNOW?

● Salvador Dali once nearly suffocated when he gave a lecture dressed in a deep-sea diver's suit. Not surprisingly, no one could hear a word that he said.

● Magritte painted unusual pictures, but he deliberately led a dull life. He followed exactly the same routine every day and filled his house with very ordinary objects.

Seated woman mending a sail, seen from the back

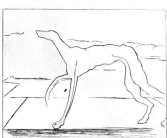

Greyhound

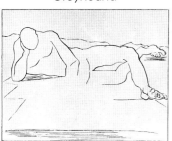

Reclining philosopher

Mandolin, fruit-dish with pears and two figs on a table

The 'one-eyed moron'

Mythological beast

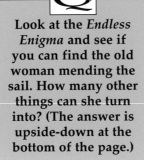

Q

Look at the *Endless Enigma* and see if you can find the old woman mending the sail. How many other things can she turn into? (The answer is upside-down at the bottom of the page.)

The Empire of Lights, 1954, by René Magritte (1898-1967)

Compared with the painting by Salvador Dali, this picture – by a Belgian Surrealist – seems perfectly normal. There's nothing obviously magical happening here. Or is there? Is this scene a night-time one – or is it showing broad daylight? What is it that makes this look like a daytime scene, and what makes us think that it is at night?

☞ The trick in this painting works because Magritte has painted the tree almost black. Objects appear black or grey both in the dark – as at the bottom of the picture – and if there is a very bright light behind them – as at the top of the picture.

Drawings for The Endless Enigma, by Salvador Dali

Dali drew six pictures that show us the different objects that we can make out in his painting The Endless Enigma. *Look back at the painting on the opposite page and see if you can find each one.*

The old woman can become the base of the fruit bowl, the nose, mouth and beard of the 'one-eyed moron', and part of the body of the mythological beast.

A

27

SEURAT'S COLOUR MAGIC

The French artist Georges Seurat (1859-1891) used a special kind of colour magic to invent a totally different way of painting.

Most painters mix different coloured paints together on a palette to get just the colour they want. But Seurat painted many of his pictures by using lots of tiny dots of different colours. As if by magic, these colours mix when you look at the painting, because the dots seem to merge into one another.

Shimmering light

Seurat hoped that, by using these dots of colour, his paintings would appear brighter, and would seem to shimmer with light. In photographs of Seurat's paintings you can tell that they are made up of dots. But the photographs are much smaller than the paintings, so you have to look at a detail to see exactly what colours these dots are.

Young Woman Powdering Herself, 1888-1890

This serious-looking young woman was Seurat's girlfriend. The dots in this painting are almost like the powder that she is using to make herself up. But the dots are also performing colour magic – her brown hair is in fact red, blue and orange!

This is a detail from the painting opposite. The man's orange-brown suit is actually made up of many different colours – including red, purple, green, blue and yellow. Can you find him in the painting?

28

COLOUR MIXING

Here are two ways of mixing the colour orange. 1. By simply mixing red and yellow paint. 2. By placing red and yellow dots next to each other. If the dots are too big, your eyes don't mix the colours. But as the dots get smaller, or you get further away, they do. Experiment by propping the book up and moving backwards until the dots in the second diagram start to merge.

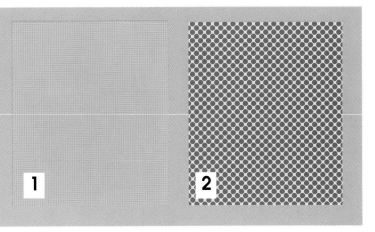

1 **2**

DID YOU KNOW?

- Colour printing works in a similar way to Seurat's paintings. All the pictures in this book are actually made up of thousands of differently coloured dots.

- The term used to describe Seurat's technique is Pointillism. This refers to the way in which he applied points of colour.

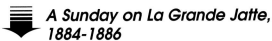

A Sunday on La Grande Jatte, 1884-1886

This large painting (206 x 306 cm) shows a sunny afternoon in a fashionable park on the outskirts of Paris, France. It was the first major picture that Seurat painted using dots.

'OP' ART

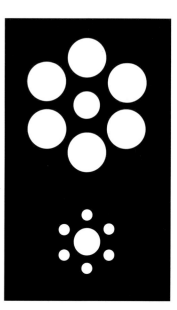

Optical art – Op Art for short – gets its name from the fact that it uses the kinds of optical illusions shown in the diagrams on these pages.

The Op Art movement was formed in the 1960s. Op Art paintings use optical illusions to create all sorts of puzzling effects. Many of these paintings seem to change as you look at them. Some of them appear to move. Just like optical illusions, Op Art paintings fool your eyes. This means that they can be extremely confusing to look at – they may even make you feel quite dizzy.

 Square of Three – Yellow and Black, 1964, by Reginald Neal (1909-1992)
How many squares can you see in this painting? You will probably find that you will have to look away after a short time!

☞ *Try concentrating on one particular area of this painting. All the parts around it will seem to wobble and flash uncontrollably.*

131-0059412 *Antique Structure, 1969, by Jean-Pierre Yvaral, also known as Jean-Pierre Vasarely (born 1934)*

This painting can change as you look at it. It can either appear as a blue grille in front of a red background, a bumpy surface with red-topped shapes, or simply a flat pattern.

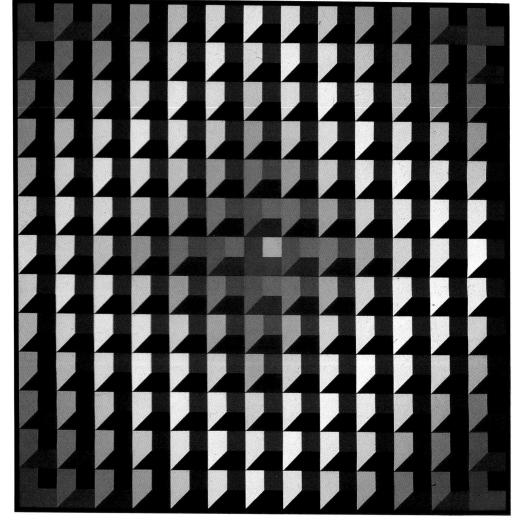

Above: This illusion has been used by several Op Artists. Look hard at this black and white grid. Grey spots seem to appear where the white lines cross. Now look straight at one point where the white lines cross – there is no grey spot at all.

Left: The long lines here look as though they are at different angles. But look along the long lines as explained below. The short crossing lines almost disappear and the long lines look parallel.

Hold the book flat, and with your eye close to the page, look along the long lines.

First look at this straight on, then look along the long lines in the direction shown by the arrow.

31

INDEX

PHOTOGRAPHIC ACKNOWLEDGEMENTS

Archiv für Kunst und Geschichte, Berlin: 17 top and cover © 1953 M. C. Escher Foundation ® Baarn - Holland. All rights reserved; 24, cover and 25 right Erich Lessing.

The Art Institute of Chicago © 1994 all rights reserved: 4 Wirt D. Walker Fund, 1949-585; 28 bottom and 29 Helen Birch Bartlett Memorial Collection 1926. 224.

Bridgeman Art Library, London: 31 top Museo de Bellas Artes, Bilbao © ADAGP, Paris and DACS, London 1994.

The Chatsworth Collection: 6.

Cordon Art: 16 both and 17 bottom © 1958 and 1960 M. C. Escher Foundation ® Baarn – Holland. All rights reserved.

Courtauld Institute Galleries, London: 28 top.

Descharnes & Descharnes, Sarl: 26 top and 27 left © Demart Pro Arte DV/DACS 1994.

Mary Evans Picture Library: 14 top and 15.

Giraudon, Paris: 7 right and title page, Musée des Beaux-Arts, 27 right Photothèque René Magritte © ADAGP, Paris and DACS, London 1994.

Museum Boerhaave, Leiden: 20.

National Art Museums of Sweden: 21 Gripsholms Slott, Stockholm.

National Gallery, London: 5 right, 12, 19.

National Gallery of Scotland: 5 left.

National Portrait Gallery, London: 18 top and centre.

New Jersey State Museum Collection: 30.

Scala: 7 left, 8 both, 9 both, 10, 11 both, 25 left.

Shell Photographic Services: 23 bottom right.